Table Of Contents

Introduction

Parenthood. We all got here by taking different paths. Young or old. Having one or four. Planned or not. We are here. Welcome to the rest of your life. Our children bring us the greatest joys we'll ever know, make us worry like never before, and introduce us to a new type of love, unconditional and so deep. They run us ragged, keep us up all night, and constantly make us think outside the box. How can I get him to take the bottle for the first time? How can I get him to take a nap? How can I get him to sleep through the night and not on me? How can I get the tantrums to stop? How can I help him learn more words so he doesn't cry and grunt to communicate anymore?

Figuring out how our kids tick is a top priority because unlike you may have initially thought, they are not little replicas of ourselves. They miraculously come out of our female bodies but are indeed their very own little people with their own ideas, their own learning styles, their own likes and dislikes, and their own communication styles. They also develop at different rates, maybe from their siblings and probably from their cousins and little friends. Sometimes this makes us doubt ourselves. Am I doing all I can to stimulate him? Is it my fault he's not walking or talking? What did I do wrong that he's not speaking yet?

It is a natural response to think it may be your own fault your child is not where you think or his pediatrician says he should be in his speech and language development. Most importantly, know that it does **not** take extraordinary circumstances for a child to learn language but it does take extraordinary circumstances for him to *not* learn language. If you talk to your child all day every day, that is enough. Sofia it's time to go to the park, let's go get your shoes. Jonathan let's go get in the bath. Hey do you want a banana or apple for snack today? The ins and out of daily life are your child's main mode of picking up speech and language skills. You do not have to take your child to the museum, the park and 5 play dates a week to learn to talk. You do not have to have multiple children for your child to learn to talk. Your child does not have be enrolled in day care or preschool to learn to talk.

On the other hand, if you do not speak to your child all day every day, and your child is neglected, he will likely not learn language. Almost 25 years ago, one of my first clients was a 3 year old who was severely neglected until the time I met him. His mother was a drug user and he was in a car seat most of his first 3 years. He made noise but knew no words when I met him. Ironically I had to first teach him to be quiet (so he could hear me and learn from me) so he could learn to talk. He was chatting away by age 5 thanks to his grandmothers dedication!!

If your child is not learning language at an expected rate, ask your pediatrician for input and advice. It may be that he isn't learning to talk for a reason. We often want our clients to attend a complete hearing test (Audiological evaluation) to be sure he's hearing everything as he should. Evaluating your child is the first step in determining why he isn't talking as we would expect. Your speech therapist may find he has a speech or language delay or disorder. She may observe behaviors indicative of a greater underlying problem like Autism if play and social interaction skills are also impaired. If one of these outcomes occurs, your pediatrician, developmental pediatrician and/or Speech Therapist should help you learn what services would be beneficial for him. Once you start speech therapy, your therapist will get to know your child and figure out his learning style, what motivates him, and she will help prioritize goals for you to help him develop his speech and language skills as much as he is capable of.

After decades of working with children in many different settings, i.e. babysitting as a teen, then working at day care facilities, then as a psychology student in schools, and clinics, I found Speech Pathology. I have now been working in the field for over 25 years and have had a wide variety of experiences which has given me such great perspective. Having such broad experiences, and running a business for over two decades, seeing little ones in different settings, school, home, and clinic, I have come to see the unique and priceless nature of working one-on-one with children, hand-in-hand with their caregivers.

My husband and I have six children between us. We've been through the ringer as many parents have with various challenges, physical and mental, over the years. Traumatic births, asthma, severe digestive issues, seizures, night terrors, surgeries, physical therapy, occupational therapy, speech therapy, anxiety, ADHD, we've experienced all of these things.

It is the culmination of these experiences, home and professional, that has brought me to the point of writing this book, a follow up to my first book, Teach Speech, A Parent's Guide: How to Teach Better Speech and Language Skills All Day Every Day. The core concepts of this book have come about through these life experiences, raising 5 children and having worked with hundreds, maybe thousands at this point, of unique little kiddos. The tenets of this book are not based on years of research with concrete numerical results but rather from decades of experience working with children with a variety of challenges and seeing what works and what doesn't. The core concept, deeply ingrained thanks to my own dad, is all about being your child's life teacher and taking advantage of every moment every day to teach your child all you can.

When you think about what your job is as a parent, what comes to mind? What are your obligations as a parent? We are here to keep our children safe and healthy but also to teach them how to take care of themselves and hopefully eventually be strong, independent people. Along the way, understanding their behavior and how it is connected to communication can help us help them! If we can learn how behavior and communication are connected, we can then learn how to teach them how to communicate more effectively and thus successfully.

Second is the concept that kids do not need flashcards to learn words. In fact, I discourage it. Children learn in their natural environments which are during *play* and during their *daily routines.* Each and every moment of your day is a learning opportunity and taking advantage of each precious moment will help you stay grounded and present and hopefully enjoy those moments as much as possible because our days go by quickly and before you know it, yes they will be grown! Those days of them sleeping on your chest, holding your hand, wanting to be with you every moment, are going to be fond memories. Taking advantage of each moment and learning how behavior and communication are connected will help you become the best life teacher you can be for your child!

In the coming chapters, I will discuss these matters in depth, so you'll end this book with a clear understanding of how behavior and communication are intertwined, how one affects the other, and how you can do your part in understanding how to not inadvertently reward negative, ineffective behaviors and communication attempts and how to make those positive, effective attempts happen more frequently. Positive effective communication sure does make for a smoother, more joyous family life. Who doesn't want that?

Chapter 1

Communication as Behavior

in Children with Developing Language

(And How We Can Shape It

With Our Responses)

What is "behavior" and how are behavior and communication connected? For the sake of *this* discussion, the term behavior is going to be used to describe an action taken by a person in an attempt to communicate his feelings, wants, needs, or thoughts in the place of words, signs or alternative forms of communication (AAC).

When a child communicates through his behavior, it can be *positive, helpful, and functional*. It can also be negative, troublesome, and ineffective. An example of a *positive, helpful, functional* behavior is when your two-year-old makes eye contact with you, looks at the item he wants, points at it, and looks back at you smiling (vs. grunting then tantruming). He's just communicated with his body that he wants a particular item and it was helpful and effective. Another example is when your 3-year old holds his hand out to accept a desired item (vs grabbing it from your hand while climbing on you). Yet another example is when your 1 year old signs "more" to request more corn for dinner (vs. screaming and reaching).

Examples of behaviors that are negative, troublesome, and/or ineffective are grunting, whining, forcefully pulling, crying, screaming, tantruming, hitting, and grabbing. Examples are when your toddler throws himself on the floor because you turned off the iPad (vs. saying "I want iPad"), when he screams because he wants the Cheerios that are too high in the cupboard (vs. pointing at them, looking at you saying "eat"), or when he grabs the toys or chips from your hand (vs. saying "please" and/or holding his hand out to accept them).

These negative behaviors may occur because your child does not yet have the words to say what he is thinking so he is expressing himself in the only way he is able and knows how. Your child *could* be talking to you instead of communicating negatively through his behaviors, if he has the ability. If he is not yet speaking, he *could* use *positive, helpful, functional* behaviors instead of negative ones like signing or gesturing.

By 2 years old, we expect children to have enough words to be able to communicate verbally. If your child has a speech and/or language delay, he needs to get his ideas across and often he uses some or many of these negative behaviors to do so. If you have concerns about your child's speech and/or language development, please do not hesitate to call your pediatrician and express your concerns. Ask for a referral for a speech/language evaluation from a qualified and experienced professional who has worked with children your child's age.

Why do parents accept (and at times inadvertently reward) negative types of communication? As parents, we just want our children to be happy. There truly is nothing more important in the big picture. We respond to our child's negative behaviors, *wanting* them to stop but in actuality, we are inadvertently rewarding them, which is making them much more likely to continue. That's right, often our responses to our child's behavior are actually making them happen again. We just do not realize how we are contributing to the problem.

Many parents who have children with challenging behaviors think their children are "difficult" or "lazy", it is what it is and there's nothing they can do about it. The fact is simple though. To a *large* extent, we *can* affect our child's behavior **by changing our reactions to them.** There are of course times when there is a limit to how we can affect or change our children's behavior. Although we may want our children to act differently or develop differently, the child is simply capable of what he's capable of. Period. So we challenge and push and see what impact we can make! If you have serious concerns about your child's behavioral development, please talk to your pediatrician immediately about it. If he/she doesn't listen or thinks you are overreacting, trust your instincts and ask to see another doctor and get a second opinion. A referral to a developmental pediatrician may be in order to determine if there is an underlying difference such as Autism Spectrum Disorder.

What often happens is that we get so caught up in the moment, wanting the child to stop crying, or screaming, wanting him or her to be happy, that we inadvertently reward the negative behavior. Where this becomes problematic is when it is an ongoing pattern and in the end, we will make no progress with the child's behavior because s/he has learned that he will get what he wants by screaming or grabbing. We are so focused on the moment that we forget to think about the big picture, that we may be "creating a monster", as they say.

My favorite analogy for this is a black sand beach in Hawaii. I just visited one recently for the first time and was obsessed with the tiny black rocks on the shore, the color was extraordinary. They were moving in such a way when the waves came that the sound caught my ear immediately. I found myself looking down for a very long time, inspecting the sizes and the amazing color. Then I remembered to look up. That was a sight indeed. The jungle came right down to the ocean on one side, palm trees lined the beach down the other side, waves were crashing, gray clouds were filling the sky as if it may rain any moment. The scene was incredible. If I had kept my head down, I would have missed it.

If you stay on today and continue to reward the negative behaviors (looking down at the black sand), you'll forget what your big picture goal truly is: a happy and expressive child who uses positive, effective communication day in and day out (a gorgeous scene from a movie with jungle, waves, trees, sounds and smells abounding).

Chapter 2

Rewards

(and How We Affect The Behavior of Others)

Any behavior that is rewarded is more likely to continue... positive or negative. In other words, if we reward (even *inadvertently*) a behavior with our *attention* or our *actions*, it will be far more likely to continue. If positive behaviors are rewarded, *they* will continue. If negative behaviors are rewarded, *they* will continue. By inadvertent, I mean we are not *trying* to reward the behavior but the end result of our reaction is a reward.

What is a "reward"? A reward is our response to a behavior that causes the behavior to be more likely to happen again. Let's walk through that explanation carefully. *"Our response to a behavior"* can be an action, a word or phrase, or something straightforward like a prize. One of the more common mistakes parents make is not realizing that giving *attention* to a behavior is often a reward. Lots of times our children are acting out because they want attention. Sometimes they are just trying to make a connection. This is the most common type of reward that is inadvertent. The child is tantruming and we feel bad for her so we hug her and pay a lot of attention to her. In so doing, we are rewarding the tantrum and it will be much more likely to happen again because it worked. She got our attention. Conversely, if a child is tantruming (and you're sure he's safe), ignoring the tantrum is usually the best response. You can let the child know, "when you're calm and ready, we can talk about the problem".

Our response, the reward, *makes the behavior more likely to happen. How we respond to our child's behavior can either make it **more** likely to occur again or **less** likely to occur again.*

Let's go back to our example of the tantruming child. If I hug him and kiss him and keep him on my lap, I rewarded the tantrum, it worked, the child got attention, so the tantrum is much more likely to happen again. If I walk away from the child when he is tantruming, he does not get any attention, and I mean even eye contact, and the tantrum will be much **less** likely to happen again because it did not work. It did not have the outcome he was looking for, of attention or getting the item or action he wanted.

If your child holds his hand out nicely to receive a snack he wants and he gets the food, he will be far more likely to hold his hand out next time around. It worked, he got the food. The behavior was rewarded with a **natural reward**, the item he wanted. No need to tell him "good job". It was a *positive, helpful, and functiona*l behavior that we want to continue and it will as long as we continue to reward it. If he screams and reaches to grab the food, and we give it to him, screaming works, so he'll keep screaming and reaching because that behavior is rewarded by getting the desired item. We have just inadvertently rewarded a behavior we really do *not* want to continue. We accidentally communicated to him by **our own** reaction that this works, keep doing it.

On the other hand, if he screams and reaches and we do not respond. We wait. Maybe he realizes this isn't working so he comes to you and hand-leads you to the cupboard and points to the food he wants. *This* is what you want to reward.

Maybe he screams and reaches, you ignore this behavior (not rewarding it), he says "eat", *then* you go to him and get him food, again you've just rewarded the behavior you *want* to continue.

Some examples of **tangible rewards** are:

- A trip to frozen yogurt for sleeping through the night five nights in a row.
- A new matchbox car for keeping his diaper dry all day.
- Dessert for eating his dinner.
- Five dollars for getting straight A's on his report card.

Those are the obvious ones but the more important ones are:
- His milk because he used the sign for milk to request it.
- Goldfish crackers because he pointed to them in the cupboard instead of crying and screaming.
- You opening the box to his favorite train set because he used words to ask you, "open box, please".

Another type of reward is *verbal praise.* A lot of parents tend to overuse praise. For instance, in the examples listed above, praise is totally unnecessary because the most important reward is the child simply getting what he wants. Let's talk about praise for a minute. There are times when praise is important to let your child know what he's doing well. That's an important point. When you do use verbal praise, stay away from the phrase "good job". Good job!   Good job! Good job! all day long gets very repetitive and boring. It conveys little meaning and after a while, loses meaning altogether. Instead, tell your child exactly what he's doing well. If you say, "nice listening", "nice sitting", "I love how you talked to me when you were upset", or "great job using your lips for that M sound", you are being very specific and now the child knows exactly what he did well. Also stay away from using the term "perfect" as being perfect or acting perfectly is definitely not the goal and we don't want the child to think it is.

Another type of reward is *attention*. If your kiddo tantrums, throws himself on the floor and you give this behavior attention, attention is a reward and he will be more likely to tantrum next time around. Attention is eye contact (watching/paying attention to him), hugs, or you talking to him.

Chapter 3

Shaping our Future

Why should we teach our child differently if they are demonstrating negative behaviors? Why not continue to accept these forms of communication and wait for his behavior to improve? What problems can they cause if they continue?

Any parent knows the pain of hearing their child cry. Oftentimes though, he is only crying because he is learning.   He is not hurt.   He is frustrated and expressing this emotion through his actions.

It's not about changing HIM, it's about changing how you DO things with him.   It's about understanding how you can affect him. It's about understanding the relationship between his behavior and your responses to his behavior.

Many toddlers go through a stage when they tantrum.   They're called the Terrible Twos for a reason. Many of our kiddos tantrum until they are 10 because they have difficulty regulating their emotions. It is important to express our feelings but as our children get older, we try to teach them more successful ways to do that.   Whether it's through talking or writing, drawing or meditating, it is very important to find out what works for your child so he can express himself!

Toddlers cannot always get what they want. It just is not real life. As adults, we cannot always get what we want. We cannot afford our dream car. We don't get the job we wish we had. We can't date the person we want because they are not interested. If we give our children every single thing they ever want right when they want it, we are leading them to think they will live a life that is not possible. If we lead them to think they can have everything they want when they want it, we often create a monster. We end up giving them cookies for breakfast, the iPad at all hours of the day, letting them stay up as late as they want, McDonald's every day. I'm exaggerating but you get the idea.

Chapter 4

Having "Just-Right" Expectations

Having the just-right expectations of your child is critical. If your child has just taken his first step, you wouldn't expect him to run across the room. In this light, it's easy to see that if he's just started learning single words, you wouldn't expect him to say sentences. If your child is capable of speaking, then you should expect him to speak to communicate. If your child is not yet capable of speaking but he is capable of signing, then you should expect him to sign to communicate. If your child isn't yet signing, but he's capable of gesturing such as holding his hand out to receive a desired item and pointing then you need to expect him to communicate in that effective, positive, functional way.

Being consistent is critical. If you accept a grunt and a reach half of the time and you expect verbalizations or talking half of the time, progress will be slow. If you expect your child to speak to communicate 100% of the time, progress will be quick. Same goes if your goal is for your child to sign or gesture to communicate. Once you've decided to adjust your expectations, go for it. Don't do it half heartedly or it will be a long road.

I call this having "just right expectations''. If your expectations are too low such as accepting a grunt and a point instead of expecting words, progress will be very slow. If your expectations are too high such as expecting your child to produce a sentence when he's only capable of saying single words, you're setting your child and yourself up for failure. It's critical to have the "just right expectations'' so that you *and* your child are set up for success. Success comes when your child has communicated clearly with you which feels good on both ends. When somebody feels successful, they feel proud and want to continue on. That's what we're going for. Remember, when he is crying, he is not hurt, he is just learning. This transformation takes time, it will not happen overnight. But the more consistent you are about your expectations, the faster it will happen, potentially within days.

When we raise our expectations, the child will get frustrated. That is expected. So expect it. For months or years, he has gotten used to being able to get what he wants using his emotions, and very easily, without putting any effort into it; without hinking, what do I need to do to get that toy or food that I want? On the one hand, it's a sweet, innocent time when we as humans, can express ourselves in the most natural ways. We scream when we're upset, we cry and laugh whenever we feel the urge, we are silly without worrying about what others think of us. Eventually we learn from our parents and teachers that some behaviors are not acceptable in our society and we start conforming. That early release of emotion is true freedom on many levels. Tantruming, screaming, grunting, and crying are not particularly enjoyable behaviors to be around and listen to though. Learning how to communicate in calm, functional ways is productive and creates a more enjoyable home environment for everybody.

Chapter 5

Creating Opportunities

for Learning and Communication

Creating opportunities for your child to learn and communicate is challenging and fun but also essential. Every moment of every day is a learning opportunity... from dressing to bathing to eating and shopping...from brushing teeth to buckling buckles to gardening and housekeeping chores. Be spontaneous and present, teach in the moment. *Playing* and *daily routines* are the most natural times for toddlers and preschoolers to learn. Take advantage of every moment.

Here are some ideas of how to do this:

1. **Fight the urge to anticipate your child's needs.** If you do this all day every day, this will make a big impact on the number of opportunities he has each day to learn and communicate with you. Every parent does this, the moment your child has difficulty with a task, you jump in and do it for him. It's a very natural process but if you fight that urge and even physically lean back a little bit to remind yourself, when your

child is having trouble performing a task, you are teaching him to be persistent. You are teaching him not to give up. It's a win-win situation. He will either work through the challenge and perform the task successfully or he will get to the point when he truly needs help, and then you target effective, functional behavior for him to either tell you he needs help or sign that he needs help or hand you the item.

Here's a common example: you're getting ready to go to the store and your child goes to put his shoes on but you know this is a pretty challenging task. You can either jump right in and put his shoes on for him or you can lean back and let him try for himself. One of two things is going to happen. He will be persistent and keep trying and he will get the shoe on by himself which is awesome *or* he will try and try and not be able to get the shoe on. What happens next is a learning opportunity. Your child might throw himself back on the floor and tantrum. In that case, you want to calmly show him the sign for help and gently tell him "oh, you need help", while simultaneously signing help. He may continue to tantrum. You can calmly tell him "when you're finished crying, I can help you put your shoe on". If he's on tile, gently move him to the carpeting so he doesn't hurt himself. Do your best to not inadvertently reward this tantrum. Remember, he's just learning, he's not hurt. Your goal is to reward functional, effective behavior. Remember, the behavior you reward is more likely to happen. So your goal here is to reward talking, signing, or gesturing.

2. **Make the set up and clean up just as important as the playing of the game.** When you're sitting down playing a game with your child, don't rush through the set up or clean up. Those are very important parts of the game where your child can learn to put toys together, learn how pieces fit together, and learn the sequence of events needed to play the game. If you are going to play with trains, and it's in a box up in the closet, ask him "where is the train set?". Have him try to find it. Ask him, "is it in the bathroom?", "Is it in the kitchen?". If he can't find it, lead him to the bedroom and then ask him, "how are we going to get it down?". Enjoy the process of finding it and setting it up. Play and enjoy for hours and then when it's time to clean up, make him an active part of that process also. If your child has a limited attention span, try to get him to finish the task

and clean up when he's done. We call this "task completion". Finish the process. Start a puzzle, finish the puzzle, put it away. It'll help keep your house clean but it will also help expand on his attention span slowly but surely.

3.   **Give choices.** This is by far the easiest way to increase the number of opportunities your child has each day to communicate with you. Incorporating this concept into your daily life does take a little bit of time so I would suggest waking up 5 to 10 minutes earlier each day and slowing your routine down a little bit whenever possible. Be present. It's tough because life pulls us in many directions at once, our minds pull us in many directions at once. Whether it is multiple kids, work, chores, spouses pulling on us, do your best to find time each day to be totally present. Don't worry about the chores or bills that need to be paid for a bit. Focus completely and wholly on your child. With work and kids, things get very hectic and you can end up rushing through your day which gives you a little opportunity to enjoy being with your precious child.

Giving your child choices is a great way not only of giving your child opportunities to communicate with you but it gives him a little bit of control in his life. We are typically telling our children where to go and what to do all day every day. This gives him a way to have some control which feels good. Obviously we're going to do this in a way where he's still safe and sound, we're not going to give him a choice if he wants to hold our hand while we cross the street or not. But each morning we could ask him, "Do you want to wear the blue shirt or the red shirt? ", "Do you want to wear the tiger shirt or the giraffe shirt? ". "Do you want to wear your red jacket or your striped jacket?" With clothes, just remember, the most important thing is for him to dress appropriately according to the weather, it really doesn't matter if his clothes match so let him have that control for his day. Same with pajamas. As long as he's dressed weather-appropriately, let him make those choices, it will feel good for both of you.

Instead of making breakfast for him every day, include him in the process. Ask him if he wants cereal or oatmeal, strawberries or bananas. It doesn't really matter what he eats for breakfast as long as he eats a healthy one. So let him have that control. It will give him an opportunity to speak, sign, or gesture, all effective, functional ways of communicating with you. In the bathtub, instead of throwing all the toys in, ask him if he wants to play with the Nemo fish or the shark, the scuba diver or the mermaid. It doesn't really matter what he plays with but if you give him choices, now he's communicating with you in effective, positive, functional ways.

4. **Sentence completion cues** are another way to elicit language from your child giving him an opportunity to communicate with you. If your child is talking, try starting a sentence and then leaving the last word off, looking at him expectantly. You can try this in books or in real life while you are out and about. For instance, pointing at the sky and saying, "Wow, that's a huge… " and look at him expectantly. Let him fill in the word, plane. While you're looking at a book, you can say, "hey that's a sheep and that's a …", looking at him expectantly. If he doesn't respond, ask him silly questions, "is it a cat? Is it a snake?" It's actually a sheep so you could just tell him if he doesn't respond, "it's a sheep, he says baba. You try it, say baba."

Chapter 6

What to expect:

Speech and Language Development

To know how to work with your child at home all day every day, you have to know what level he is functioning at right now. Then you will need to know what the next steps are and what is reasonable to expect. Knowing his age is one thing, but knowing what developmental level he is at is another thing and is much more important. In other words, if your child is three, but developmentally he is at an 18-month level, you would not work on 3-year-old skills, but rather 18- to 24-month skills. Conversely, your child might be two but speaking at a 3 1/2 year-old level, with hundreds of words and five- and six-word sentences. First, let's discuss some definitions

"**Speech**" refers to **pronunciation**. In the Speech Pathology field, we call it "**articulation**". All three of these terms refer to how *clearly* your child speaks. Does your child produce all of his sounds clearly or does he have a lisp? Does he omit sounds in words like saying "-top" for stop or a "ca-" for cat? Does he substitute one sound for another such as saying "fwee" for three (substituting "f" for "th" and "w" for "r")?

Sounds develop in a fairly predictable pattern so we expect children to master certain sounds by certain ages. That being said, every child has his strengths and challenges whether it's being good at riding a tricycle and not so good at swimming or being good at gymnastics but not so good at playing nicely with his friends. With speech it's the same way. While we expect children to use certain sounds by certain ages, one child might master complex sounds like "r" or "ch" at age 2 while another child might not master these sounds until age five, which is also considered "within the average range". It's always important to remember that there is a wide range of "normal" when it comes to speech and language in toddlers and preschoolers. The milestones that we will go over in this book are minimum expectancies. So you might find that your child has far exceeded some of the milestones listed for his age. If he has not mastered the milestones listed for his age, there are many things you can do at home, as the person who knows him best, to help him move forward more quickly. Of course, asking your pediatrician for a referral for a speech and language evaluation may also be in order.

The term "intelligibility" refers to how well people understand what your child is saying. Can mom understand what he is saying 80% of the time but strangers only get 20% of what he says? It's normal for parents to understand their children better than strangers but it's the latter that we use to judge a child's true intelligibility. Again there is a range of normal and the milestones you will find listed here are minimum expectancies.

Chapter 7

Speech Milestones

6-18 mon:
From 6-12 months: babbling with repetitive sounds (baba, dada, mama) throughout day with early sounds such as "m,n,b,d" and a variety of vowel sounds. From 12-18 months, complex sound combinations are expected (baga, digy) with varying intonation, called "jargoning". *By 18 months, toddlers should be readily and spontaneously imitating sounds and words.*

By age 2:
50% intelligible, should be using "m,n,p,b,t,d,h" in addition to vowels (e.g., "ah,ee,oh,oo,uh,ih,a")

By age 3:
80% intelligible, should be using above sounds + "k,g,f", all vowel sounds and vowel combinations

---

By age 4:
90% intelligible, should be using above sounds + blends which are 2 consonants in a row such as Stop, Star, Black, Drop, etc. ("s,l,r" may be distorted such as with a lisp, or saying a "w" sound for a "r,l" sound)

By age 5:
100% intelligible
Above + "l,r,th" should be mastered

Chapter 8

Language Milestones

Receptive language refers to how well your child understands language spoken to him; how well he follows directions, understands various vocabulary terms, and how well he understands questions. This area of development is also called **auditory comprehension**.

Expressive language refers to your child's ability to express himself verbally; how large his vocabulary is, how often he is combining words into *novel/unique* phrases and sentences, and how accurate his grammar (word order) and morphology (word endings) are.

Receptive Language Expectancies:

By 12-14 mon:
Responds to name
Recognizes words
Follows simple directions

By age 2:
Points to many body parts
Follows novel directions
Points to named pictures

By age 3:
Follows 2-step directions
Listens to stories
Understands opposites

By age 4:
Answers simple "Who?", "What?", "Where?" questions

By age 5:
Pays attention to short stories and answers questions
Understands most of what is said to him

Expressive Language Expectancies:

By 12-14 mon:
Complex babbling
First words

By age 2:
At least 50 words
Combining words into novel combinations

By age 3:
100s of words
"Conversational"
Using 3- and 4-word utterances

By age 4:
Talks about past events
Uses 4- and 5-word utterances on average

By age 5:
Uses adult-like grammar
Uses sentences with much detail
Communicates with children and adults easily

If you have any concerns about your child's speech or language development, talk to your pediatrician. Feel free to call Seven Bridges Therapy at 510-250-9199.

Made in the USA
Columbia, SC
14 October 2024